YOUR KNOWLEDGE HAS VALUE

Bibliographic information published by the German National Library:

The German National Library lists this publication in the National Bibliography; detailed bibliographic data are available on the Internet at http://dnb.dnb.de .

Imprint:

Copyright © 2011 GRIN Verlag, Open Publishing GmbH
Print and binding: Books on Demand GmbH, Norderstedt Germany
ISBN: 9783668374430

This book at GRIN:

http://www.grin.com/en/e-book/350704/on-the-importance-of-a-long-term-approach-to-peace-processes

Anna Scheithauer

On the Importance of a Long-term Approach to Peace Processes

On the Inadequacies of Zartman's „Ripe Moment" to overall Conflict Resolution and the Social Psychological Dimensions of Ethnic Conflicts

GRIN Publishing

GRIN - Your knowledge has value

Since its foundation in 1998, GRIN has specialized in publishing academic texts by students, college teachers and other academics as e-book and printed book. The website www.grin.com is an ideal platform for presenting term papers, final papers, scientific essays, dissertations and specialist books.

Visit us on the internet:

http://www.grin.com/

http://www.facebook.com/grincom

http://www.twitter.com/grin_com

ON THE IMPORTANCE OF A LONG-TERM APPROACH TO PEACE PROCESSES

On the Inadequacies of Zartman's „Ripe Moment" to overall Conflict Resolution and the Social Psychological Dimensions of Ethnic Conflicts

Anna Scheithauer

Wien, Juni 2011

TABLE OF CONTENTS

INTRODUCTION

This paper is set out to give a possible account of why so many peace processes concerning intra-state ethnic conflicts have produced „no war, no peace" situations, hence states of negative peace where risks for resumed fightings are high, rather than an actual resolution fostering mutual understanding and recognition involving society at large.

The first section of this assignment is designed to point out the necessity to resolve conflicts by peaceful means as well as of conflict transformation and, thereby, deals with the wide-spread assumption first introduced by Zartman that conflicts require a "ripe moment" as the ideal entry point for eg. mediators to reach a peace agreement among the belligerents which I will argue only leads to a peace settlement and thus, more often to a flawed peace than to the conflict's resolution. John Paul Lederach's approach of cultivating peace and Ramsbotham's ideas of conflict transformation both stressing the cruciality of a long-term approach to peace processes shall underline my argumentation.

The second part then explores the fundamentals of the social psychological aspects of ethnic conflicts reflected upon so well by Herbert Kelman who builds upon Burton's research concerning the dimension of deep rooted conflicts - as ethical conflicts usually can be described! - emphasising human needs and fears over interests, since they can be seen as the root cause for the inadequacy of Zartman's theory of the "ripe moment". Moreover, the concept of work-shops designed by Kelman as a feature of track II diplomacy in conflict resolution shall serve as a successful example for an alternative in a long-term approach to peace processes.

Altogether, it is to notice that the paper is based on the constructivist assumption of the ethnic concept in contrast to the primordialist thought. Furthermore, Zartman's "ripe moment", should not in anyway be discredited in its contribution to conflict resolution as it can serve as a valuable turning point. However, it should not be seen as *the* solution but rather as an initial/accompanying step in a long-term process that is essential for a sustainable peace.

Finally, when taking these considerations in mind the core element needed in addition for a successful peace process is political and societal will in order to really overcome "no war, no peace" situations on the long-term!

ON THE IMPORTANCE OF A LONG-TERM APPROACH TO PEACE PROCESSES

ON THE INADEQUACIES OF ZARTMAN'S „RIPE MOMENT"

Intra-state ethnic conflicts reaching an international dimension can be considered a phenomenon of the 20th as well as 21st century often threatening the maintenance of international peace and security. The UN Charter, therefore, stresses decisively in Chapter VI the importance of pacific settlements of disputes whereby Article 33(1) points out that "The parties to any dispute, the continuance of which is likely to endanger the maintenance of international peace and security, shall, first of all, seek a solution by negotiation, enquiry, mediation, conciliation, arbitration, judicial settlement, resort to regional agencies or arrangements, or other peaceful means of their own choice."[1]

Conflict resolution to solve ethical conflicts has taken many forms so far but has most often lead to what we would describe as a flawed peace. Roger Mac Ginty argues that these "no war, no peace" situations occur in three forms: 1. where "[...] a violent conflict has largely been contained in a geographic region of a larger state" (eg. the "two Ugandas"), 2. "[...] where a peace accord has been reached between the main antagonists in a civill war but the implementation of the accord becomes stalled and fails to move towards a truly transformative peace", 3. where "[...] a peace process becomes established through a ceasefire and a routine of inter-group meetings."[2]

---

1 Charter of the UN. "Chapter VI: Pacific Settlement of Disputes",
http://www.un.org/en/documents/charter/chapter6.shtml , June 2011
2 Mac Ginty, R (2010) "No war no peace: Why so many peace processes fail to deliver peace."

Hence, the obvious inadequacies can be seen in the mere achievement of a peace settlement through ceasefire agreements and with it the lack of conflict transformation as such, as well as through separating warring ethnic groups rather than integrating society by fostering mutual understanding and recognition.

At this point I would like to argue that Zartman's so often applied theory of a "ripe moment" as embodied by a hurting stalemate is a causation factor for such an "no war, no peace" situation if not accompanied by a long-term overall approach to establishing peace. Zartman claims that conflicts can best be tackled when an opportunity in form of a "hurting stalemate" in terms of eg. a change in power relations, a military setback or the failure to impose a unilateral outcome, presents itself. This is usually referred to as the "ripe moment" where most often mediation efforts set in.[3]

So why is it that Zartman's exclamation for the need of a "ripe moment" can be considered insufficient? Most of all, this concept experiences as pointed out above practical limitations. John Lederach remarks that ripeness is more a rearview mirror rather than a forward-looking skill orientation suggesting linearity of process and a predictive capacity. Usually it is only in retrospect that we define situations as ripe ones.[4] The second implication of this assumption is that ripeness pretty much is in the eye of the beholder as "[...] ripeness is more often than not something perceived by outsiders with the luxury of dispassionate facts and factors. In the midst of week-to-week and month-to-month emergencies people rarely see their situations as 'ripe' for peace."[5]

Furthermore, Lederach claims that ripeness focuses more on the mediator as the actor than as mediation as a process involving multiple people, functions and roles which resembles more a harvest whereby the negotiated agreement represents the fruit rather than a cultivation involving real changes in people and perceptions.[6] This very well can

---

International Politics Vol. 47(2), p. 147/148
3 Bercovitch, Jacob (1997). "Mediation in International Conflict" In: William Zartman/Lewis Rassmussen, "Peacemaking in International Conflict", Washington, p. 145
4 Lederach, John Paul (1999), "Cultivating Pace: A Practitioner's View of deadly Conflict and Negotiation" In: Preparing for Peace. New York. p. 31/32
5 Ebd., p. 33
6 Ebd., p. 33/34

be linked to Mac Ginty's argument in point 2. on the previous page as then "[...] local actors have difficulty achieving a sense of ownership of the peace accord: its implementation becomes something that is done to them rather than a process in which they are full participants."[7]

In this respect, Ramsbotham et al. argue as well that the "hurting stalemate" model is too focused on the power relationship between the parties and does not sufficiently consider changes within the parties nor the context. Moreover, they point out that there often are situations which represent "hurting stalemates" but do not lead to successful negotiations/outcomes like it has been the case during the Cyprus conflict. Also the authors stress that we need to distinguish between ripeness for negotiations to begin and ripeness for them to succeed initiating the idea of a "ripening process" rather than the requirement for a "ripe moment" as a sudden event.[8]

Considering this argumentation I particularly want to emphasise the idea of ripeness as "[...] a complex process of transformations in the situation, shifts in public attitudes and new perceptions and visions among decision-makers."[9] which goes together with the approach of conflict transformation besides conflict settlement and conflict management as tools of conflict resolution, embodying in my opinion the most crucial task to accomplish a positive peace.

In this view, Burton, Azar and Curle define five generic transformers of protracted conflict whereby context transformation relates to the social, regional and international context in which conflicts are embedded and that often lead to their continuation. Probably the most often cited example for such a transformation is the end of the Cold War. However, local structures might be resistant to change on a regional or international level so that a change in the set of actors and their incompatible goals is required (eg. shift from an asymmetric to a symmetric relationship).[10]

---

7 Mac Ginty, R (2010) "No war no peace: Why so many peace processes fail to deliver peace." International Politics Vol. 47(2), p. 152
8 Ramsbotham, Oliver et al., "Peacemaking" In: "Contemporary Conflict Resolution". Cambridge. p. 167
9 Ramsbotham, Oliver et al., "Peacemaking" In: "Contemporary Conflict Resolution". Cambridge. p. 167
10 Ebd., p. 163

A precondition for this step can be seen in the necessity of actor transformation by redefining directions through for example "[...] a change of actor, a change of leadership, a change in the constituency of the leader, or adoption of new goals, values or beliefs."[11] With it goes the transformation of issues when there is for example a change of positions or when certain matters lose salience or new ones are on the rise. But at the heart of change is the fifth aspect and that is personal/group transformation involving changes in values. This can be best exemplified by a leader of an oppressive government agreeing to accepts his opponent(s) into the government.[12]

These transformations can be considered to need accompaniment by the international community or simply third parties, might they be from in- or outside, in the form of "[...] ongoing presence motivated by an interest in supporting a sustainable change process built on making opportunity available for genuine change motivated from within but not under obligation or external time frames."[13] Hence, there are no quick-fixes to long-standing violent ethnic conflicts without risking a relapse into violence because at the root of such conflicts there usually is a "knot of problematic relationships" representing different interests and diverging world-views so that conflict resolution must be concerned with more than dividing issues taking a comprehensive long-term approach specifically addressing the underlying social and psychological dimensions to bring about the required transformations.[14]

THE SOCIAL PSYCHOLOGICAL DIMENSIONS OF ETHNIC CONFLICTS

Having now touched on the social and psychological domain it needs to be explained that particularly the debate on ethnic identity in context of ethnically motivated conflicts is spurred by two contrasting views. The primordialists hold that ethnicity is a permanent feature of a group embodying "[...] a primordial bond between the members of a 'natural' community which precedes modern nation-states and class systems and

---

11 Ebd., p. 163
12 Ebd., p. 163/164
13 Lederach, John Paul (1999), "Cultivating Pace: A Practitioner's View of deadly Conflict and Negotiation" In: Preparing for Peace. New York. p. 36
14 Ramsbotham, Oliver et al., "Peacemaking" In: "Contemporary Conflict Resolution". Cambridge. p. 164

transcends them." stressing the idea of a common origin and common rituals.[15] The constructivists, on the other hand, view ethnic identity as socially constructed, which adapts to changing contexts and environments and, thus, underlies constant change.[16] Thus, whatever is artificially constructed can be de-constructed!

The constructivist view can be considered as the more contemporary one supported by the international community to large extent, and needs to be taken as the underlying perception upon which this paper is based upon as primordialist thought would not consider social psychological transformations as relevant or even a credible/possible aspect for the resolution of ethnic conflicts.

In order to reflect upon Kelman's thoughts to innate aspects of parties to an ethnic conflict we first need to take into consideration Burton's work on deep-rooted conflicts which predates Kelman's research and, thus, provides the basis. John Burton discusses the importance to differentiate between interests and needs in deep-rooted ethnic conflicts the former offering the possibility of being bargained about which the latter do not provide for. He there refers to Paul Sites who placed power realistically not with the authorities but with individuals and groups which pursue ontological needs. In this respect, he articulates that the root causes of ethnic conflicts can be seen in both the denial of human needs and distributive justice and that conflicts might be protracted unnecessarily due to the translation of inalienable needs into interests for mere bargaining reasons.[17]

However, he also stresses as these ontological needs for eg. security, identity and human development are universal ones and their fulfilment is not depended on limited resources, non-zero-sum outcomes are indeed possible. In this regard he also points to the danger of temporary settlements - as already mentioned in previous paragraphs of this assignment – without tackling the underlying issues as well as the importance to

---

15 Stavenhagen, R (1998) „Ethnic conflicts and their impact on international society". International Social Science Journal, Vol. 50 (157), p. 438

16 Toth, R (2010) Zwischen Konflikt und Kooperation: Fünfzehn Jahre Friedenskonsolidierung in Bosnien und Herzegowina. Wiesbaden: VS Verlag für Sozialwissenschaften, Kapitel 2.1 „Krieg – Bürgerkrieg – ethnopolitische Konflikte", p. 16

17 Burton, John W. (1987), "Resolving Deep-Rooted Conflict". A Handbook, Virginia, p. 15/16

asses the costs of ignoring such non-negotiable needs and highlights in this connection the decisive role of facilitated conflict resolution with its focus on problem-solving.[18]

Herbert Kelman then explores further the aspect of ontological needs in ethnic conflict situations where particularly psychological factors seem to be pervasive especially with sight to the relationship of individuals to society respectively the social system as such. He, therefore, is in line with Burton when he identifies ethnic conflict as "a process driven by collective needs and fears" in addition to "an inter-societal process, not only an interstate or intergovernmental phenomenon", "a multifaceted process of mutual influence, not only a contest in the exercise of coercive power" and as "an interactive process with an escalatory, self-perpetuating dynamic [...]"[19]

Ethnic conflict defined as an inter-societal process takes account of the happenings within society such as internal divisions leading to intra-group conflicts in the parties of a conflict which can constrain political leaders heavily, or the forming of coalitions across the conflict lines which is a wonderful example for the social construction of such an ethnic identity as well as for the importance and possibility of transformations in structures, attitudes and relationships. Conflict as a multifaceted process, on the other hand, takes account of various forms of mutual influence, not just coercive power to achieve one's ends. This can take the form of a mixture of threats & inducements, mutual assurance in terms of acknowledgements, symbolic gestures or confidence building measures, responsiveness to the other's concerns & sensitivity to the other's constraints, careful adherence to the principle of reciprocity etc. facilitating the recognition of the conflict as a shared problem.[20]

Moreover, ethnic conflict defined as an interactive process with an escalatory, self-perpetuating dynamic relates to the aspect that the natural course conflicts take tend to deepen them through socio-psychological barriers respectively processes that promote

---

18 Ebd., p. 16-18/21
19 Kelman, Herbert C. (1997), "Social Psychologic Dimensions of International Conflict" In: W. Zartman/Lewis Rasmussen, "Peacemaking in International Conflict", Washington, p. 193/194
20 Ebd., p. 199-208

conflict such as mirror images and self-fulfilling prophecies fostering mutual de-legitimisation and de-humanisation.[21] With these processes Kelman differentiates between normative and perceptional ones whereby the former relate to "[...] social processes that provide expectations, support, and pressure to hold on to the conflict, affirm it and engage in conflict behaviour", while the latter refers to "[..] cognitive processes that help to interpret and organise conflict-related info".[22]

Further, Kehlman suggests that such conflict norms and images have their roots in ontological needs and fears, are features both on the level of political leadership and the general public, and are the cause for the escalatory, self-perpetuating dynamic as mentioned above.[23]

Normative processes particularly relate to the formation of collective moods where historical traumas usually serve as the points of reference for current happenings; the mobilisation of group loyalties where studies show that people tend to be more risk-averse to achieve gains but far more risk-acceptant to avoid losses willing to make huge sacrifices for national security and safety/survival; decision-making processes relying on established procedures and technologies rather than exploring new/non-violent options as well as on the concept of group think in order not to endanger the group's cohesiveness through "inadequate" decision-making; negotiation & bargaining processes with a focus on zero-sum thinking; and a vested interest in the status quo as a result of profit, power and status motives.[24]

Perceptual process in contrast to the normative ones relate for example to the formation of mirror images where the parties have positive self-images where harmony between leaders and followers is assumed but negative enemy-images believing that the enemy's unity is completely artificial. Also it typically is believed that "[...] the other side's aggressiveness is inherent in its nature, in its ideology, in its system, in its religion, in its national character [...]" while "[...] one's own side is entirely reactive and

---

21 Kelman, Herbert C. (1997), "Social Psychologic Dimensions of International Conflict" In: W. Zartman/Lewis Rasmussen, "Peacemaking in International Conflict", Washington, p. 208-210
22 Ebd., p. 211
23 Ebd., p. 211/212
24 Ebd., p. 212-222

defensive."[25] which in the literature is termed a *fundamental attribution error.* Also the resistance of images to contradictory information can be classified under the rubric of perceptional processes. Change always faces some resistance might it be for reasons of attitudes, selectivity, consistency, attributions or self-fulfilling prophecies. However, inconsistent information can often be "[...] an important instigator of change in attitude and behaviour provided the information is compelling and challenging and situational forces motivate the person to seek out new information."[26] so that strong beliefs of the unchangeability of the enemy can be overcome.

What has come to the forefront is the complexities of an ethnic conflict situation involving more levels of society than just the parties leader(s) as is assumed with Zartman's model of a "ripe moment" which focuses more on the power relations and, thereby, leaves out other important aspects.

Given this comprehensiveness of ethnic conflicts, the question then arouses if there are appropriate tools available for effective conflict resolution. Yes there are, and an example for it is facilitated conflict resolution in form of the interactive problem-solving work-shop concept focusing on exactly this intersection between social psychology and conflict resolution introduced by Herbert Kelman who applied this model successfully at various stages of the Israel-Palestine conflict which lead to the Declaration of Principles serving as the basis of the Oslo Accords in 1993.[27]

These work-shops involve small groups with representatives of the parties in their capacity as private citizens (= track II diplomacy) that closely interact, try to identify barriers to peace and try to understand each other's concerns, needs, fears, priorities and constraints. The work-shop concept contributes to conflict resolution by the development of cadres (actor transformation), by allowing for substantive inputs such as changes in relationship (structural transformation) and by changing the political atmosphere in terms of a shift from a zero-sum to a win-win situation (issue

---

25 Kehlman, Herbert C. (1997), "Social Psychologic Dimensions of International Conflict" In: W.
Zartman/Lewis Rasmussen, "Peacemaking in International Conflict", Washington, p. 223
26 Ebd., p. 228
27 Kelman, Herbert C. (1995), "Contributions of an Unofficial CR effort to the Israeli-Palestinian
Breakthrough" Negotiation Journal, Volume 11, Number 1, Plenum Press: New York & London, p. 19-26

transformation). So, work-shops pretty much function as a microcosm of the larger, as a laboratory for producing inputs into the larger system, as a setting for direct interactions, enable coalition building across conflict lines and serve as a nucleus for a new relationship. Of course, the idea of the work-shop is one of various concepts within conflict resolution but one of a few really taking account of the complex dimensions, including particularly the social psychological ones, of ethnic conflicts.[28]

CONCLUSION

It has become obvious now through this argumentation that situations of negative peace respectively "no war, no peace" situations often are a result of a quick-fix in terms of a peace settlement not involving all parties to the conflict and not taking into consideration the complexities of an ethnic conflict situation. What lurks behind this outcome is Zartman's theory on a "ripe moment" failing to acknowledge the fact that peace needs to be cultivated and nourished; from what experience has shown peace is not a quick harvest!

Therefore, positive peace requires true changes in context, situation, actors, and the individuals/groups and not just in issues that have usually been mistaken for interests instead of deep-rooted ontological needs and fears, hence making use of inappropriate means such as bargaining techniques and pursuing inadequate zero-sum outcomes instead of creating mutual understanding & recognition and promoting win-win outcomes.

In this regard, the comprehensiveness of ethnic conflicts can be directly related to the social psychological dimensions of individuals in relation to their society so that ethnic conflicts can actually be defined as driven by human needs and fears, are to be considered inter-societal, are indeed multifaceted and exhibit an escalating, self-perpetuating dynamic driven by normative and perceptual processes. But considering the concept of ethnic identity as socially constructed there are ways of facilitated conflict

---

28 Scheithauer, Anna. "Herbert C. Kelman – Problem-Solving Workshops", class notes of the "Negotiation, CR and Peacekeeping" class at the International University, Vienna, February 2011

resolution (eg. Kelman's work-shop concept) that can be seen as a valuable means to provide a real solution to ethnic conflicts.

The social psychological dimension, thus, draws our attention to the need for a long-term approach to a peace process requiring real transformations in structures, actors contexts and so forth in order to really resolve a conflict. If society as such is not ready for acceptant of peace, a peace agreement/settlement between the belligerents will only lead to a negative peace being prone to actions of spoilers and other war-time beneficiaries. Therefore, peace settlements should be seen as an initial step of a long-term peace process fostering a self-sustaining peace rather than the only or final step!

BIBLIOGRAPHY

Bercovitch, Jacob (1997). "Mediation in International Conflict" In: William Zartman/Lewis Rassmussen, "Peacemaking in International Conflict", Washington.

Burton, John W. (1987), "Resolving Deep-Rooted Conflict". A Handbook, Virginia.

Charter of the UN. "Chapter VI: Pacific Settlement of Disputes", http://www.un.org/en/documents/charter/chapter6.shtml , June 2011

Kelman, Herbert C. (1995), "Contributions of an Unofficial CR effort to the Israeli-Palestinian Breakthrough" Negotiation Journal, Volume 11, Number 1, Plenum Press: New York and London.

Kehlman, Herbert C. (1997), "Social Psychologic Dimensions of International Conflict" In: W. Zartman/Lewis Rasmussen, "Peacemaking in International Conflict", Washington.

Lederach, John Paul (1999), "Cultivating Pace: A Practitioner's View of deadly Conflict and Negotiation" In: Preparing for Peace. New York.

Mac Ginty, R (2010) "No war no peace: Why so many peace processes fail to deliver peace." International Politics Vol. 47(2).

Ramsbotham, Oliver et al., "Peacemaking" In: "Contemporary Conflict Resolution". Cambridge.

Scheithauer, Anna. "Herbert C. Kelman – Problem-Solving Workshops", class notes of the "Negotiation, CR and Peacekeeping" class at the International University, Vienna, February 2011

Stavenhagen, R (1998) „Ethnic conflicts and their impact on international society". International Social Science Journal, Vol. 50 (157).

Toth, R (2010) Zwischen Konflikt und Kooperation: Fünfzehn Jahre Friedenskonsolidierung in Bosnien und Herzegowina. Wiesbaden: VS Verlag für Sozialwissenschaften, Kapitel 2.1 „Krieg – Bürgerkrieg – ethnopolitische Konflikte".

YOUR KNOWLEDGE HAS VALUE

- We will publish your bachelor's and
  master's thesis, essays and papers

- Your own eBook and book -
  sold worldwide in all relevant shops

- Earn money with each sale

Upload your text at www.GRIN.com
and publish for free